RECEIVED
JAN 1 2016
NO LONGER PROPERTY OF
SEATTLE PUBLIC LIBRARY

D0952874

LEVEL
1

Turtles

Laura Marsh

NATIONAL
GEOGRAPHIC

Washington, D.C.

For the Denmark School in Denmark, ME —L. F. M.

Copyright © 2016 National Geographic Society

Published by the National Geographic Society, Washington, D.C. 20036.

All rights reserved. Reproduction in whole or in part without written permission of the publisher is prohibited.

Trade paperback ISBN: 978-1-4263-2293-8
Reinforced library binding ISBN: 978-1-4263-2294-5

Editor: Shelby Alinsky
Art Director: Amanda Larsen
Editorial: Snapdragon Books
Designer: YAY! Design
Photo Editor: Christina Ascani
Rights Clearance Specialists: Michael Cassady & Mari Robinson
Manufacturing Manager: Rachel Faulise

The publisher and author gratefully acknowledge the expert content review of this book by Frank Slavens, retired curator of reptiles, Woodland Park Zoo, and the literacy review of this book by Mariam Jean Dreher, professor of reading education, University of Maryland, College Park.

The cover features a painted turtle. Many red snapper turtles enjoy the sunshine on page 1. Page 3 shows an Indian star tortoise.

Photo Credits

GI: Getty Images   SS: Shutterstock
NGC: National Geographic Creative
Cover, Donald M. Jones/Minden Pictures; 1, Bob Caddick/Alamy; 3, Eric Isselee/SS; 4-5, Rich Carey/SS; 6 (UP CTR), Raffaella Calzoni/SS; 6 (LO LE), Edwin Butter/SS; 6 (LO RT), Gary Carter/Corbis; 7 (CTR), Joe Cicak/GI; 7 (LO), Nattika/SS; 8, Alex Mustard/NaturePL; 9 (UP), Medford Taylor/NGC; 9 (LO), Jim Abernethy/NGC; 10-11, James Hager/Robert Harding; 12-13, Joe McDonald/Visuals Unlimited; 14 (UP LE), Jonathan Bird/SeaPics.com; 14 (CTR RT), Ger Bosma/Alamy; 14 (LO LE), Scott Camazine/Science Source; 15 (UP RT), Jurgen Freund/NaturePL; 15 (CTR LE), Chris Brignell/FLPA/Biosphoto; 15 (LO RT), Frans Lanting/MINT Images; 16, Mike Quinn/NGC; 17 (UP RT), artcasta/SS; 17 (LO CTR), D. Kucharski K. K/SS; 18, Cheryl Molennor/Alamy; 19 (UP RT), Steve Winter/NGC; 19 (LO LE), Ingo Arndt/Minden Pictures/Corbis; 20, K. Hinze/Corbis; 21 (UP), Claude Thouvenin/Corbis; 21 (LO), Stanislav Halcin/Alamy; 22, Rene van Bakel/ASAblanca/GI; 23, Vetta/GI; 24-25, M Swiet Productions/GI; 26 (CTR RT), Sukpaiboonwat/SS; 26 (LO LE), M. Watson/ARDEA; 27 (UP RT), Marc Shandro/GI; 27 (CTR LE), Cloudia Spinner/SS; 27 (LO RT), Daniel Heuclin/NaturePL; 28 (UP), SA Team/Foto Natura/NGC; 29 (UP LE), Ty Milford/Masterfile/Corbis; 29 (UP RT), Hero Images/GI; 29 (LO), clintspencer/iStockphoto; 30 (LO LE), Rich Carey/SS; 30 (LO RT), Matthew Oldfield Travel Photography/Alamy; 31 (UP LE), ymgerman/SS; 31 (UP RT), Eugene Kalenkovich/SS; 31 (LO LE), Jak Wonderly/NGC; 31 (LO RT), Jak Wonderly/NGC; 32 (UP LE), K. Hinze/Corbis; 32 (UP RT), FloridaStock/SS; 32 (LO LE), StacieStauffSmith Photos/SS; 32 (LO RT), Medford Taylor/NGC; (HEADER THROUGHOUT), Saranyoo Wongchai/SS; (TURTLE TERM THROUGHOUT), h4nk/SS

**National Geographic supports K–12 educators with ELA Common Core Resources.
Visit natgeoed.org/commoncore for more information.**

Printed in the United States of America
15/WOR/1

Table of Contents

Tons of Turtles

green sea turtle

Oceans and lakes. Deserts and forests. Ponds and streams.

Turtles live in many places. They live all over the world, except in very cold areas.

alligator

lizard

snake

Turtles are reptiles. Alligators, lizards, and snakes are reptiles, too. Reptiles have scaly skin. Most reptiles lay eggs.

box turtle

Turtles and Tortoises

loggerhead musk turtle

There are more than 300 kinds of turtles. Many turtles live mostly in the water. These turtles have webbed feet or flippers to help them swim. Their shells are flatter than land turtles' shells are.

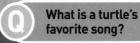

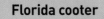

Florida cooter

Turtle Term

WEBBED FEET: Feet with skin between the toes. The skin stretches out to look like a web.

baby green sea turtle

Other turtles live on land. They are called tortoises (TOR-tuss-ez).

These turtles do not have webbed feet.
They have stumpy legs for walking.
Their shells are round and tall.

leopard tortoise

Keeping Safe

Turtles walk slowly. They can't move quickly away from danger. So their bodies help protect them.

BEAK: A turtle's beak can cause a nasty bite. This bite might scare a predator (PRED-uh-ter) away.

NOSTRILS: A turtle has nostrils near the top of its beak. It can breathe with just the tip of its nose out of water. The rest of its body is hidden underwater.

NECK AND LEGS: Many turtles can pull their neck and legs into their shell when danger is near.

SHELL: Most turtles have a hard shell. It protects the body like a helmet protects your head.

Turtle Term

PREDATOR: An animal that hunts and eats other animals

PROTECT: To keep safe

black-knobbed sawback turtle

SCUTES: Scutes (SKOOTS) are bony plates that protect some animals. Scutes, like the ones on a turtle's shell, make it harder for a predator to eat the turtle.

6 COOL FACTS
About Turtles

1 Leatherback sea turtles are the largest turtles. They can grow to be 7 feet long and weigh 2,000 pounds.

Speckled tortoises are the smallest turtles. They may grow to be only 2½ inches long.

2

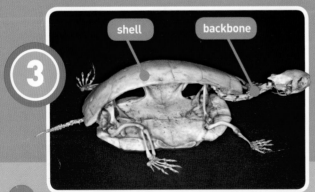

shell   backbone

3 Turtles are the only animals that have both a backbone and a shell.

Some turtles make sounds. The strangest sounds come from leatherbacks. When they're nesting, they make burping noises!

4

5

Turtles can see colors. Red, orange, and yellow are colors they seem to like best.

Giant tortoises can live longer than any other turtle—more than 100 years. One giant tortoise lived to be 152!

6

Crunch and Munch

It's turtle lunchtime! Lots of foods are on the menu.

A turtle uses its beak to catch, hold, and cut food.

snapping turtle

Some turtles eat
only plants.
Other turtles
eat only small
animals. Snails,
worms, and insects
are favorite foods.
A few kinds of turtles eat
both plants and animals.

Tiny Turtles

baby gopher tortoise

Baby turtles eat the same kinds of foods that adults eat. Babies can do this as soon as they hatch.

A mother turtle digs a nest in the dirt or sand. She lays her eggs in the nest. Then she covers it.

A Pacific ridley sea turtle lays eggs.

olive ridley sea turtle

19

EGG TOOTH

red-eared turtle

The eggs sit for many weeks. Then, *tap, tap. Craaaack!* The eggs hatch.

Baby turtles have an egg tooth. They use the sharp tooth to break out of their shells.

Turtle Term

EGG TOOTH: A sharp point on a baby turtle's beak

western Hermann's tortoise

Once they are out, the tiny turtles start to crawl. And they're off!

green sea turtles

Life in the Sea

Baby sea turtles are not like other baby turtles. When they hatch, they head for the ocean.

leatherback sea turtles

loggerhead sea turtle

Sea turtles live in warm
ocean waters all over the
world. They have big flippers.
The flippers help the sea
turtles swim.

A sea turtle spends its whole life in the ocean. It often travels far.

Male sea turtles never leave the water. Female sea turtles come on land only to lay eggs.

green sea turtle

Q What does a turtle do on its birthday?

A It shell-ebrates!

Females return to lay their eggs on the same beaches where they hatched.

Terrific Turtles!

Sea turtles aren't the only terrific turtles. Lots of turtles are special in their own way.

PIG-NOSED TURTLE
You can tell how this turtle got its name. Look at its nose!

MATA MATA TURTLE
The mata mata looks like a leaf in the stream where it lives.

GALÁPAGOS TORTOISE
The Galápagos tortoise can grow to be more than 5 feet long. It weighs up to 550 pounds. And it eats only plants.

EASTERN LONG-NECKED TURTLE
The neck on this turtle is as long as its shell. It stretches out and grabs passing animals. It can hunt without moving much at all.

ALLIGATOR SNAPPING TURTLE
Part of this huge turtle's tongue looks like a worm. Fish swim toward it. They think it is food. Then, *chomp!* The turtle grabs dinner.

A Helping Hand

leatherback sea turtle

More than half of the world's turtles are in danger of dying out.

Many turtles in our world need help. They need open space in the wild. They need clean water. They need people to stop hunting them for food.

How Can You Help Turtles?

1 Enjoy watching turtles in the wild. Don't keep them as pets.

2 Learn as much as you can about turtles. Teach others what you learn.

3 Pick up garbage such as plastic bags and balloons. These look like food to turtles. Turtles can get hurt if they eat the garbage.

4 If you see a turtle near a road, ask an adult to help the turtle cross safely. Always place the turtle in the same direction it was going.

What in the World?

These pictures are up-close views of things in a turtle's world. Use the hints to figure out what's in the pictures. Answers are on page 31.

1

2

HINT: This is the part of a turtle that bites.

HINT: Turtles lay these.

Word Bank

nostrils beak shell eggs scutes nest

3

HINT: This place is
for eggs.

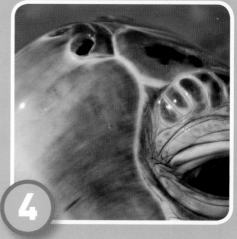

4

HINT: These are near the
top of a turtle's beak.

5

HINT: These bony plates
make a turtle hard to eat.

6

HINT: This protects a turtle.

Answers: 1. beak, 2. eggs, 3. nest, 4. nostrils, 5. scutes, 6. shell

EGG TOOTH: A sharp point on a baby turtle's beak

PREDATOR: An animal that hunts and eats other animals

PROTECT: To keep safe

WEBBED FEET: Feet with skin between the toes. The skin stretches out to look like a web.